What Was It Like Before Electricity?

Acknowledgments

Executive Editor: Diane Sharpe
Supervising Editor: Stephanie Muller
Design Manager: Sharon Golden
Page Design: Simon Balley Design Associates
Photography: Beamish, the North of England Open Air Museum: pages 10, 12, 14; ET Archive: cover (bottom), page 8; Mary Evans Photo Library: cover (left and top), pages 9, 13, 16, 17, 18, 20, 23; Ann Ronan Photo Library: pages 11, 19, 22, 24—25; Zefa: page 27.

Library of Congress Cataloging-in-Publication Data

Bennett, Paul, 1954-
    What was it like before electricity?/Paul Bennett; illustrated by Carolyn Scrace.
      p.   cm. — (Read all about it)
    Includes index.
    ISBN 0-8114-5734-6 Hardcover
    ISBN 0-8114-3786-8 Softcover
    1. Technology — History — Juvenile literature.   2. Household appliances — History — Juvenile literature.
[1. Technology — History.   2. Household appliances — History.]   I. Scrace, Carolyn, ill. II. Title.
III. Series: Read all about it (Austin, Tex.)
T48.B48 1995
609—dc20

94-28575
CIP
AC

What Was It Like Before Electricity?

Paul Bennett

Illustrated by

Carolyn Scrace

STECK-VAUGHN
C O M P A N Y
ELEMENTARY • SECONDARY • ADULT • LIBRARY

Her house is really interesting. It has so much old stuff in it.

The house is so old. It was built before there was electricity. There are still old gas lamps on the wall. Can you see them?

Show us around the house, Great-Grandma!

We want to see all your old junk.

It's not old junk. There are many old memories here. Come with me, and I'll tell you about some of them.

When I was a girl, we used oil lamps
because we didn't have electric lights.
I went to bed by candlelight.

That must have
been spooky!

That's not a tennis racket. It's a carpet beater. When I was young, there were no machines to clean carpets.

I had to hang our carpets on a clothesline and beat them with that. I got very dusty!

I bet it's easier now that you have a vacuum cleaner.

Nearly every room had a fireplace.
We burned wood or coal to keep warm.
We did all our cooking on a wood or
coal stove, too.

Sometimes we would use a kerosene heater.
You filled the tank at the bottom with
kerosene and then lit the wick. Our house
always smelled like kerosene.

Well, do you see that old tub over there? That was our washtub. Every Monday, my mother used to wash all the clothes by hand.

First she heated the water over a coal fire. Then she stirred the clothes with a wooden paddle called a dolly.

That sounds like hard work to me!

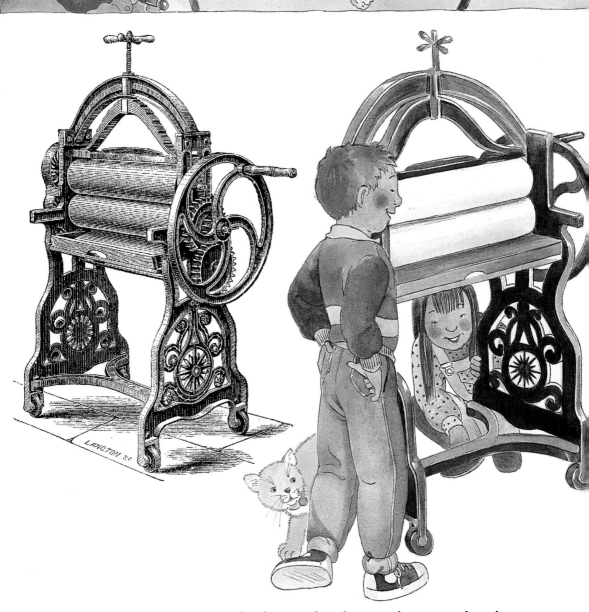

Then she squeezed the clothes through that machine with the two rollers. It's called a wringer. If you got your fingers caught in it, you knew it!

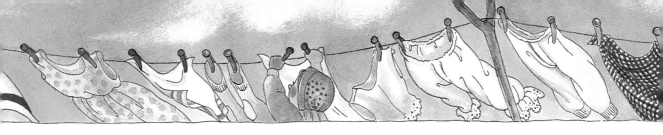

My mother hung the clothes on the line or by the fire to dry. Our house was always full of wet washing.

They are flatirons. We had to heat them
up on top of a coal stove. My mother
would spit on them to see if they were hot.

Hey! Look at this funny old record player!

That's my phonograph. I used to play music on that and dance to it when I was a child.

You had to wind it up. That trumpet thing made the sound. I've still got some old records somewhere. We could try it.

May I wind it up?

Was there really no TV when you were young, Great-Grandma?

Television hadn't been invented when I was your age. After school I used to play hopscotch or roll a wooden hoop. Here's an old one.

In the evening I would play the violin or the piano, or maybe I'd read a book.

I had a doll with a china head. Of course, we didn't have any toys that needed batteries.

My brother had some
wind-up toys, and we
both liked to play
marbles.

I like playing marbles.

Well, trains were very different in my day. When I was a girl, we used to travel on steam trains. They were very noisy and dirty.

Clouds of smoke came billowing out of the smokestack as we chugged along.

Yes, it has made my life easier, but we still had good times in those days.

Can you name the things on this page? The answers are on the last page, but don't look until you have tried naming everything.

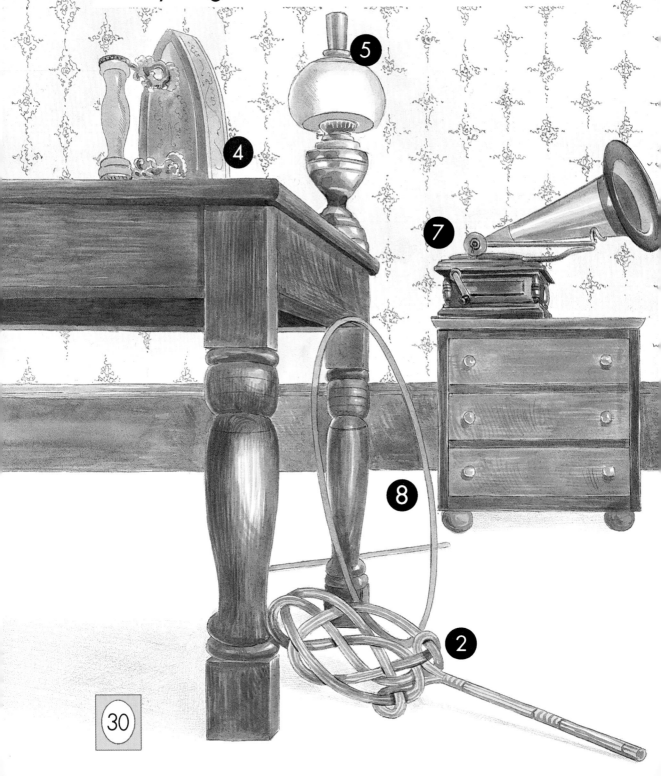

Index

Answers: 1. Kerosene heater 2. Carpet beater 3. Washtub 4. Flatiron
5. Oil lamp 6. Wringer 7. Phonograph 8. Hoop